MW01139313

THIS BOOK IS DEDICATED TO
THE CHILDREN AROUND THE WORLD!

Children
in the
BIBLE

By Cristina Marques

SCANDINAVIA

Children in the Bible
© Scandinavia Publishing House
Drejervej 15,3 DK - Copenhagen NV Demark
Tel. (+45) 3531 0330
www.scanpublishing.dk
info@scanpublishing.dk

Text: Cristina Marques
Illustrations: Belli Studio
Graphic design: Gao Hanyu
Translation: Ruth Marschalek, Lissa Jensen

Printed in China
ISBN: 9788772478081

All rights reserved. No part of this book may be reproduced or utilized in any form or by any means, electronical or mechanical, including photocopying, recording, or by any information storage and retrieval system, without the permission in writing from the publisher.

Children
in the
BIBLE

By Cristina Marques

SCANDINAVIA

INTRODUCTION

Jesus said, "Become like little children." *The Children of the Bible* series brings attention to the littlest of Jesus' flock. Each of these characters has an inspiring story to tell. God has used their lives to teach the world about his love. As you read these stories aloud, remember God's image inside every child's spirit. The simplest stories sometimes hold the greatest power. May these stories be the beginning of a lifelong love of the Bible for your children. It holds treasures to find for young and old alike.

CONTENTS

Isaac

(GENESIS 21:1-4, 22:1-19)

Abraham and Sarah were getting old, but they wanted to have a child. God told Abraham they would have a son. Sarah thought it was impossible. "We're too old!" she laughed. But God kept his promise, and she gave birth to a happy boy. They named him Isaac.

Abraham adored Isaac. He taught him all about God's love. He taught him that God doesn't just love us. God wants us to love Him, too. One night God said to Abraham, "Take your son Isaac by the hand. Hike up to the mountain top. I want you to sacrifice Isaac to show that you love me."

Abraham felt sad. He didn't want to sacrifice Isaac. But he trusted God. He saddled his donkey, and brought along two servants. He took Isaac to the mountain top just as God had asked.

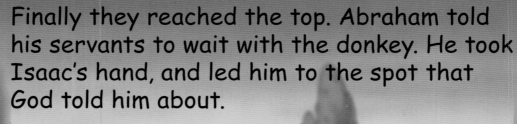

Finally they reached the top. Abraham told his servants to wait with the donkey. He took Isaac's hand, and led him to the spot that God told him about.

15

Isaac looked at his father, and asked, "What now, Daddy? Where is the lamb?" Abraham told Isaac that God would provide the lamb. Then he sighed. His heart was heavy.

18

Abraham knew Isaac would have to die. But he obeyed God. He tied Isaac to a bundle of wood. He lifted his knife, and then an angel appeared. "Stop," the angel shouted. "Don't hurt Isaac!"

The angel smiled. "Now God knows how much you love Him. You obeyed His word even though it meant giving up your only child. Be happy! God will protect you and Isaac forever."

21

Abraham and Isaac were happy. They offered a ram up to God. Then they worshiped him there on the mountain top.

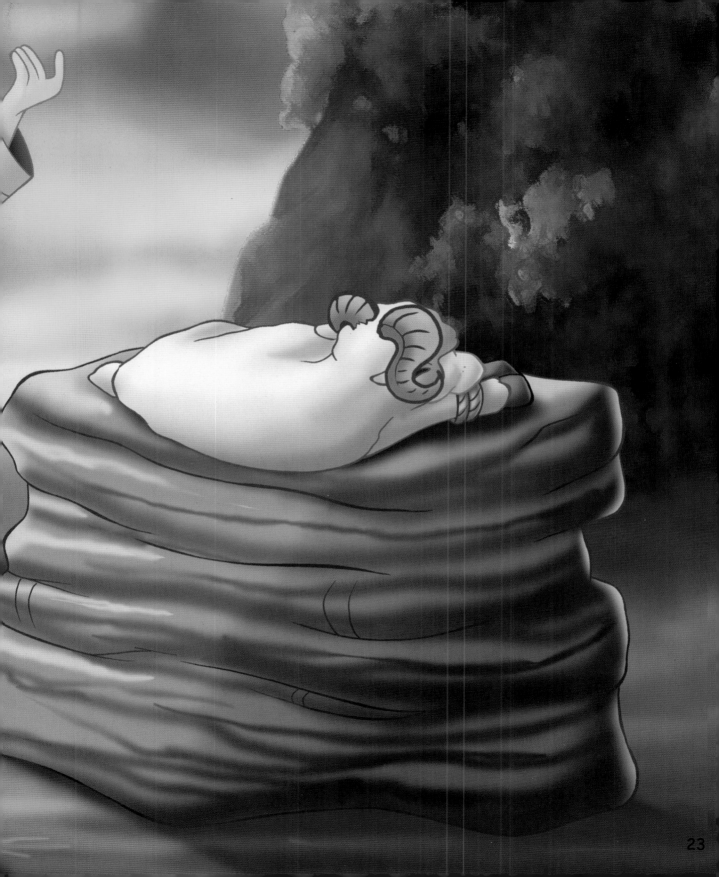

Isaac never forgot that day. Abraham obeyed God. God blessed them both. Abraham tickled Isaac. Isaac laughed and felt God's love all around him.

ISAAC - TRUST

Isaac's story can be difficult to understand, even for adults. But the heart of this story is about trust. Sometimes we can't understand why people do certain things. Even God can be difficult to understand! Abraham didn't understand why God wanted him to sacrifice Isaac. Isaac didn't understand why his father took him up to the mountain. But both Abraham and Isaac put their trust in the Father. Sometimes we don't have all the answers. But when we trust, we show we believe inside our hearts. Just like Isaac, our faith will pay off. God rewards those who trust in him.

Miriam

(EXODUS 2:1-9)

Miriam was a brave girl. Most people have heard the story of her brother, Moses. But if it wasn't for Miriam, Moses might never have had a story to tell!

At the time of Miriam, the Hebrews lived in Egypt. They were ruled by a cruel king. He ordered every Hebrew baby boy to be drowned. It was a scary time for the families.

Miriam was a little girl when her brother Moses was born. Her mother was afraid Moses would be stolen and killed. She laid Moses in a basket, put the basket in the river, then watched it float away.

Miriam loved her little brother Moses. She wanted to make sure he would be okay. So she hid in the bushes by the river and watched the basket float by.

Then the Egyptian princess came down to wash herself in the river. She saw Moses' basket floating on the water. She sent a maid to fetch it. Baby Moses was crying inside. "It's a little Hebrew boy!" the princess said.

34

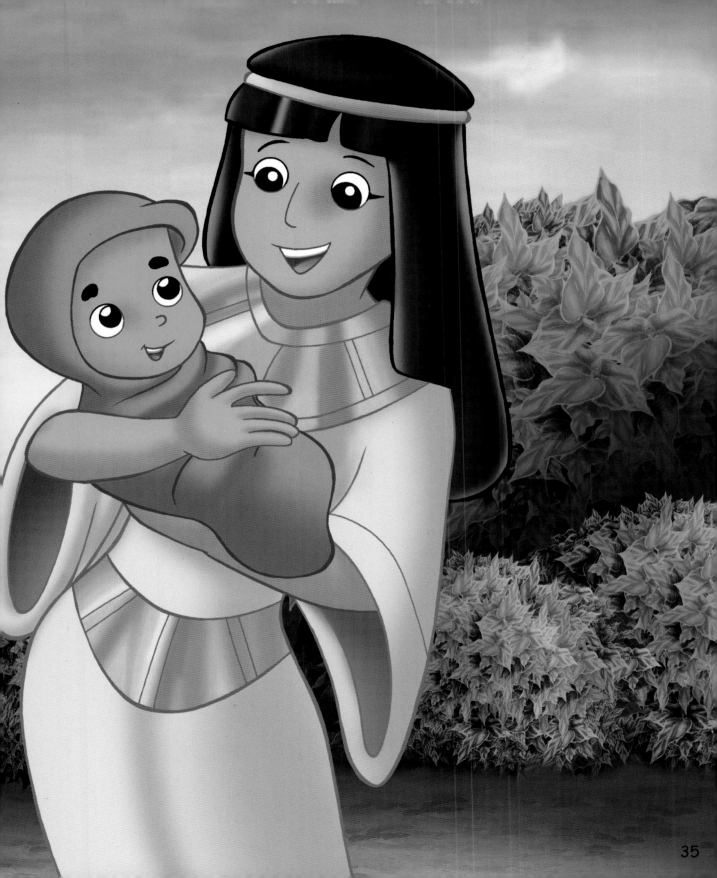

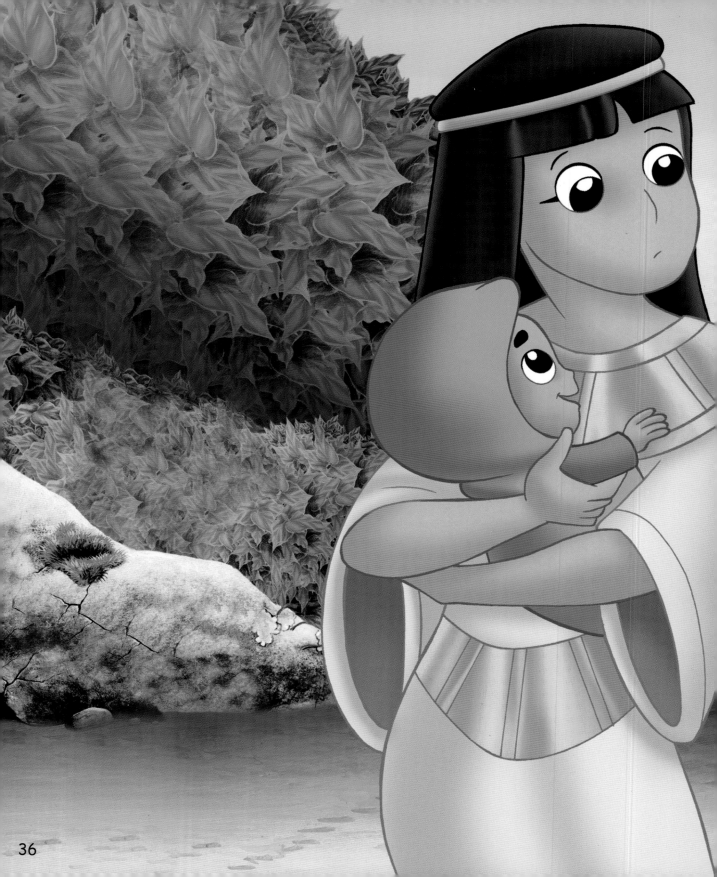

Miriam stepped out of the bushes when she heard what the princess said. Her heart was racing. The princess was surprised to see the little girl. Then Miriam asked, "Princess, shall I find a woman to nurse this baby for you?"

The Princess said, "Yes!" So Miriam got her own mother and took her to the Princess. "Take this boy and nurse him," the Princess said. "When he is older I will take him to live in my palace!"

Miriam and her mother took care of Moses when he was growing up. They taught him about God. They raised him with love until it was time for him to go live in the palace.

When Moses grew up, even after living in the palace, he never forgot his people. One great day he led the Hebrews out of Egypt to freedom. The cruel king could not hurt them anymore. Miriam was proud of her brother. She loved him and never left his side just like that day by the river.

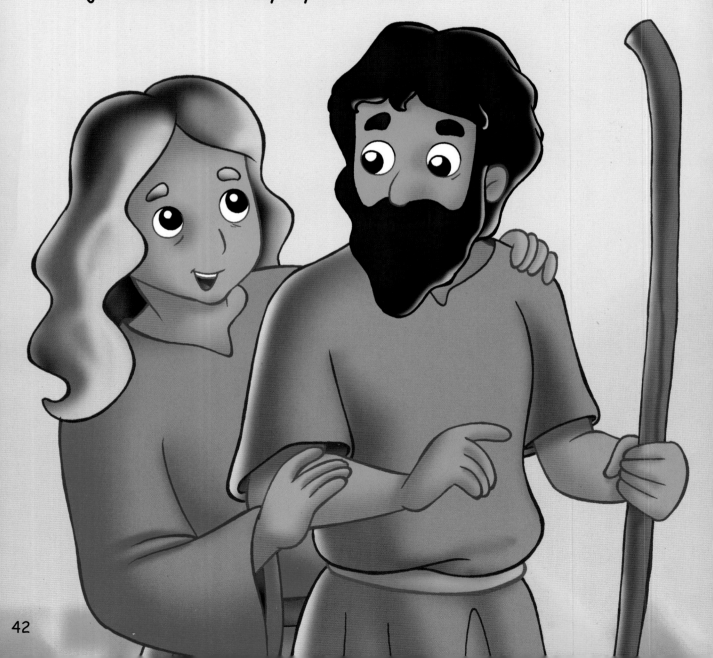

MIRIAM - INTELLIGENCE

Miriam loved her brother Moses. She wanted him to be safe. When her mother put Moses in the river to hide him, Miriam did not leave his side. And when Miriam saw the princess holding Moses, she thought of a plan. She would have her mother nurse the baby for the princess! Miriam's intelligence meant that Moses was safely brought back home again. God gave us intelligence to solve problems. He gave us intelligence to help one another, too. When we use this gift, we bring glory to God.

Moses

(EXODUS 2:1-10)

Moses, a Hebrew boy, was born in Egypt. It was a dangerous time. The Hebrew people were slaves. The king of Egypt had sent out an order that all Hebrew baby boys must be killed.

Moses' mother was frightened. She knew the soldiers would find Moses. So she put him in a basket. She took him to the river and let him float away. But Miriam, Moses' sister, hid behind the grass. She watched over Moses.

A little while later, the Egyptian princess came down to bathe in the river. She spotted something on the water. "What could it be?" she asked her maids. When she opened the basket, she saw little Moses inside crying.

48

The princess rocked the baby in her arms. She was enchanted by him but had no milk to feed him. At that moment, Miriam stepped out of her hiding spot. She told the princess, "I know a good nurse. She will care for the baby for you!"

The princess loved Moses. She happily agreed with Miriam's plan. Miriam went and got her own mother. Miriam's mother raised Moses until he was old enough to live with the princess.

Moses had a wonderful childhood. His mother taught him about God's love. She also taught him about God's promises for his people. But soon the time came for Moses to leave. He was old enough to live at the palace.

The years went by, and Moses was taught by many Egyptian teachers. But he never forgot his own people. His love for God was strong. He became a leader among the Hebrew people.

Moses became so well-loved that the king became jealous. He wanted to get rid of Moses. Moses escaped and hid out among his people, the Israelites. God watched over him. He told Moses about his plan to free Israel from slavery. And God chose Moses as their leader.

Just as God promised, Moses led his people to the Promised Land. During the journey, God gave Moses the Ten Commandments. The Commandments taught his people about right and wrong. Moses was a faithful servant of God until the end of his days. His love of God was as strong as stone.

MOSES - DETERMINATION

Moses spent many years growing up in a palace. He could have anything he wanted. But Moses didn't care about all that stuff. He was determined to be a servant of God. He became unpopular among the Egyptians. Still Moses was determined to help God. He knew God had a plan to set Israel free.

Moses wanted to be a part of God's plan. When that time came, he left his comfortable life behind. We can set our minds to do something good. We can decide that we won't give up. Maybe that means being a friend to someone. Maybe that means helping out with chores. Whatever it is, don't give up! Show determination, just like Moses.

Naaman's Servant Girl

(2 KINGS 5:1-14)

Naaman was the captain of the Syrian army. On one of the raids by the army, a little girl was taken from Israel. She was brought back to Naaman's home. There she became a servant to Naaman's wife. She felt at home in the family.

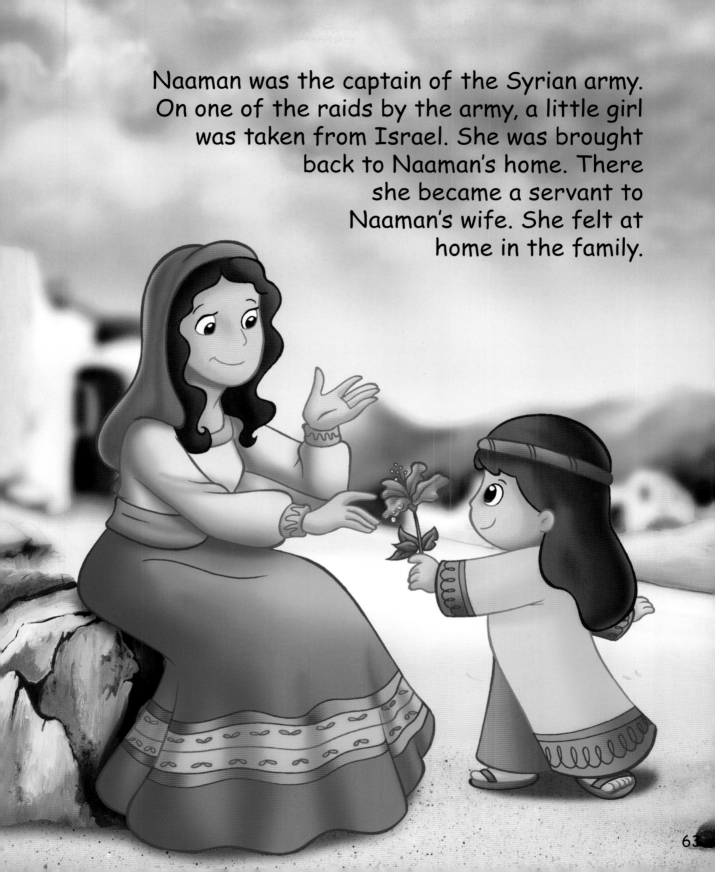

Naaman was a brave man and a wonderful fighter. But he was unhappy because he had a disease called leprosy. His wife's little servant girl felt terrible about it. She didn't like to see people hurting.

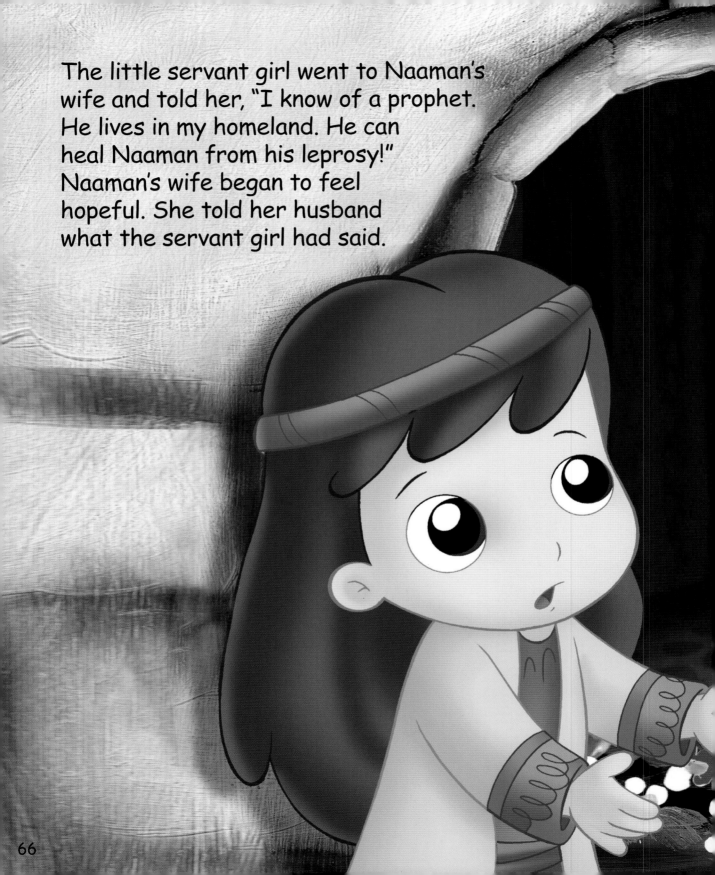

The little servant girl went to Naaman's wife and told her, "I know of a prophet. He lives in my homeland. He can heal Naaman from his leprosy!" Naaman's wife began to feel hopeful. She told her husband what the servant girl had said.

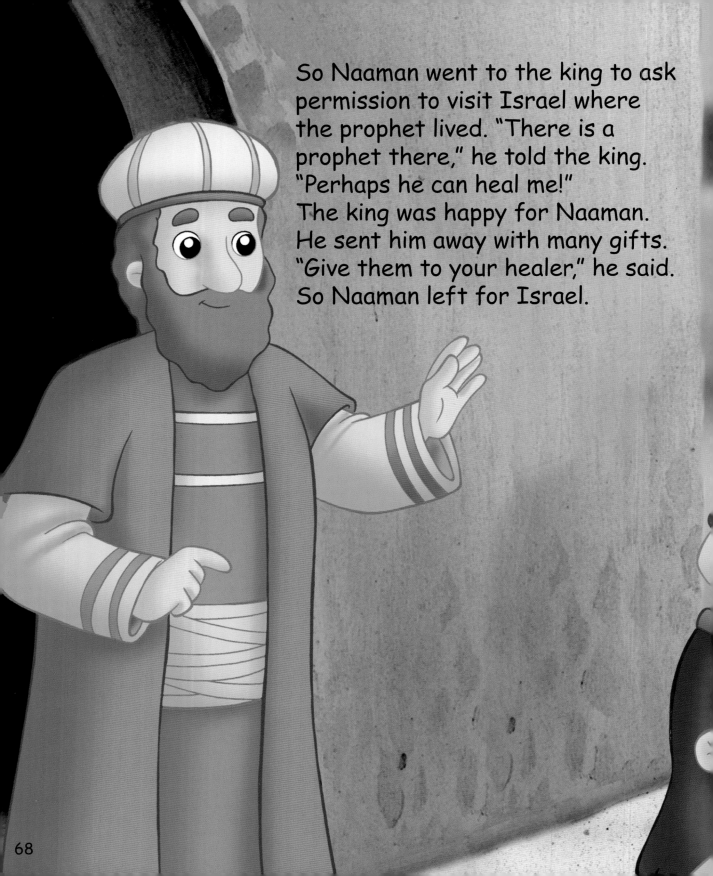

So Naaman went to the king to ask permission to visit Israel where the prophet lived. "There is a prophet there," he told the king. "Perhaps he can heal me!"
The king was happy for Naaman. He sent him away with many gifts. "Give them to your healer," he said. So Naaman left for Israel.

When Naaman arrived, the prophet Elisha sent a messenger out to him. The messenger told Naaman to wash in the Jordan River seven times. But Naaman didn't listen because he was angry.

"Where is Elisha?" Naaman growled. "I've come all this way. I thought Elisha would be here. I thought he'd heal me right away!" Naaman stormed off in a rage.

The servants took Naaman aside. They calmed him down. "Don't you want to be healed?" they asked him. Naaman nodded. He went down to the Jordan River. There he washed himself seven times. When he stepped out of the water, his leprosy was gone!

Back home the little servant girl was happy for Naaman. She took care of him the best that she could. Every day he grew stronger.

The little servant girl
knew God had healed
Naaman. She had shared
her love of God by telling
him about the prophet of
God. And God had worked a
miracle that wonderful day!

NAAMAN'S SERVANT GIRL - COMPASSION

The little servant girl was a foreigner in a strange land. She was taken by Naaman's army and made to be a servant. But she was not angry or spiteful. When she saw Naaman in pain, she wanted to help him. This is what compassion is all about. She did what she could do. She told Naaman and his wife about God's healing power and the prophet Elisha. Naaman went to the prophet Elisha and was healed. When we see people who are hurting, we can show them we care. We can be an instrument of God's love just like the little girl.

Samuel

(1 SAMUEL 1:9-28 / 3:1-19)

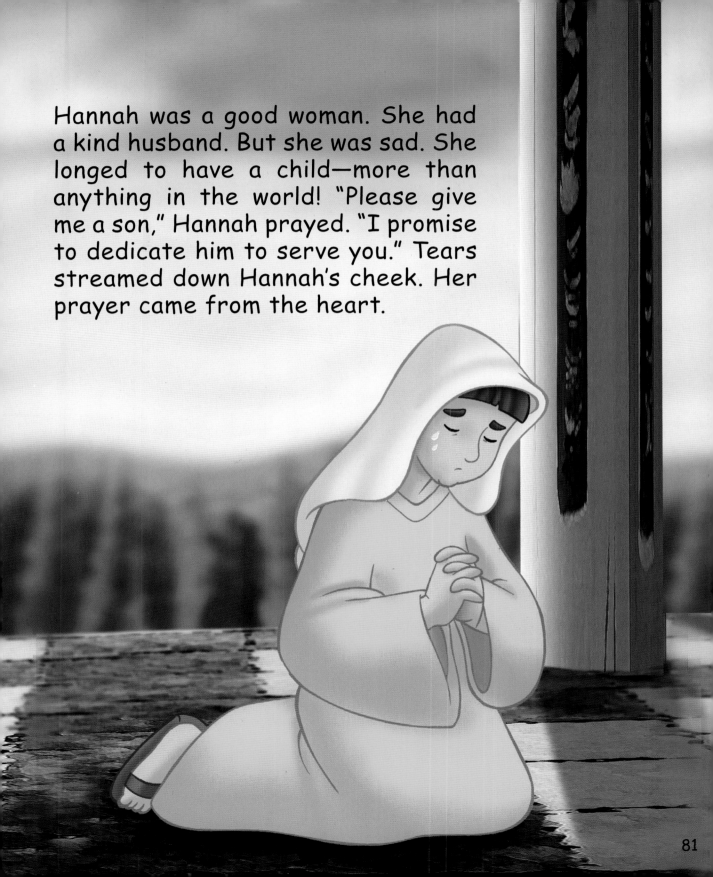

Hannah was a good woman. She had a kind husband. But she was sad. She longed to have a child—more than anything in the world! "Please give me a son," Hannah prayed. "I promise to dedicate him to serve you." Tears streamed down Hannah's cheek. Her prayer came from the heart.

God answered Hannah's prayer.
He gave her a child. She was
overjoyed! At last she,
too, was a mother.
She named her son
Samuel, which
means "because I
asked the Lord
for him."

Hannah adored Samuel. She spent all her time playing with him. She taught him how to walk and talk. She cuddled him. She told him stories. But she hadn't forgotten her promise. She had promised God to let Samuel grow up in the church. Now the time had come for him to go live with the other servants of God.

Hannah took Samuel to the priest, Eli.
"The Lord answered my prayer for a child," she told the priest. "And now I have promised to dedicate him to God. Will you let him live here in God's house?"

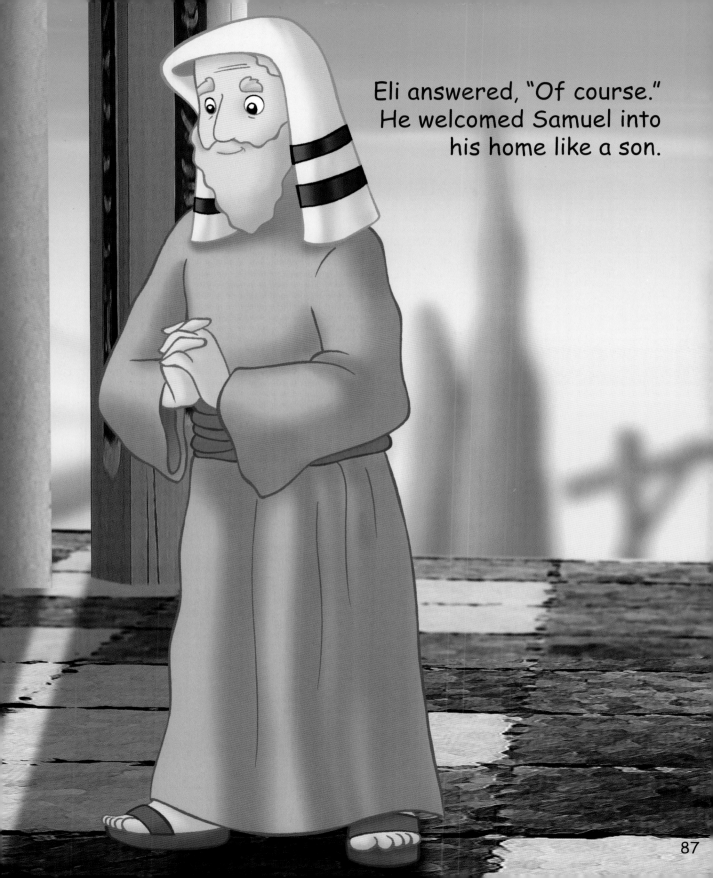

Eli answered, "Of course." He welcomed Samuel into his home like a son.

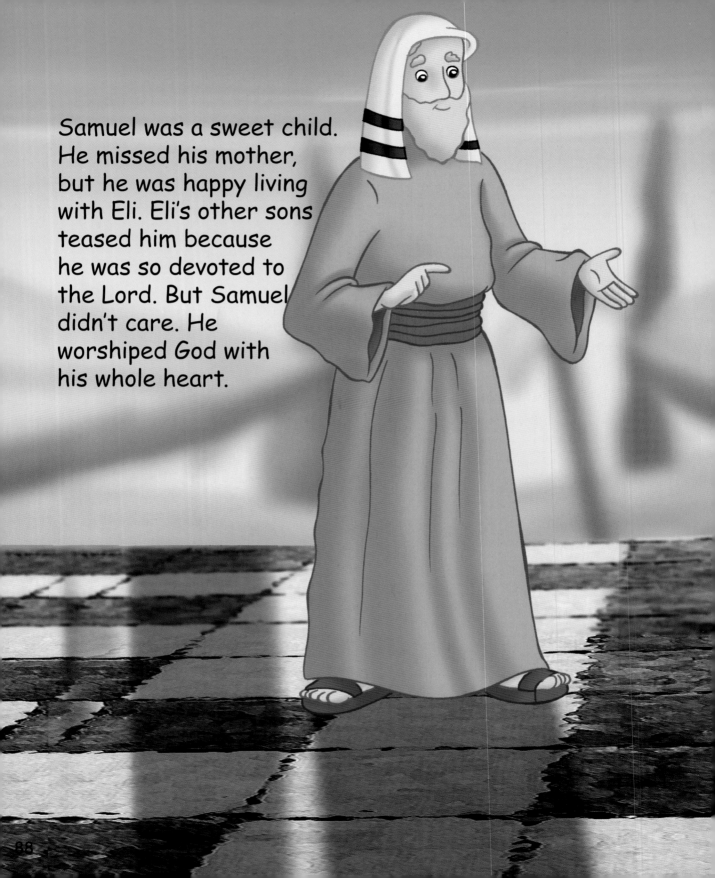

Samuel was a sweet child. He missed his mother, but he was happy living with Eli. Eli's other sons teased him because he was so devoted to the Lord. But Samuel didn't care. He worshiped God with his whole heart.

One night Samuel was sleeping. He heard a voice call, "Samuel!"

Samuel got up and went to Eli. "Did you call me?" he asked him.

"No," Eli said. "Go back to bed."

But again, Samuel heard a voice call, "Samuel! Samuel!" So Samuel went to Eli again.

"I didn't call you," Eli said. "Go lie down."

"Samuel!" a voice called again.

Samuel went to Eli. This time Eli told him, "When you hear the call, say: 'Speak, I'm listening.'" So Samuel lay down again.

"Samuel!" the voice called. Samuel answered, "Speak, I'm listening!"

Then God told him, "Eli's sons have been cruel. And Eli has done nothing to stop them."

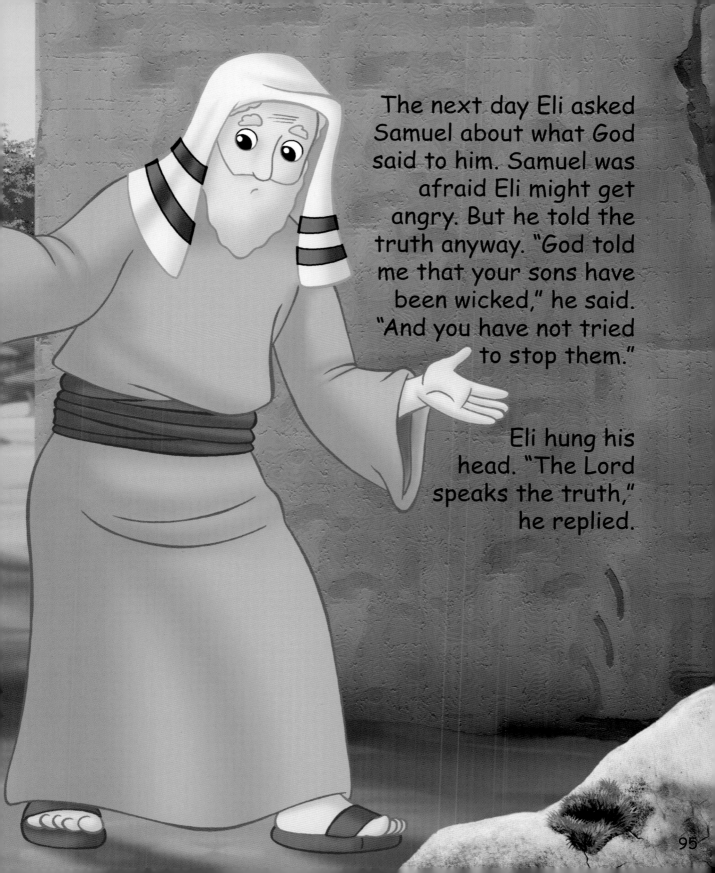

The next day Eli asked Samuel about what God said to him. Samuel was afraid Eli might get angry. But he told the truth anyway. "God told me that your sons have been wicked," he said. "And you have not tried to stop them."

Eli hung his head. "The Lord speaks the truth," he replied.

Samuel grew up to be a priest just like Eli because he learned to listen to God. He never turned his back on God. He taught other people about the importance of listening. Sometimes God calls when we least expect it! Just like Samuel, we can say, "Yes, God, I am listening!"

SAMUEL - DEVOTION

Hannah dedicated her child to serve God. But it was Samuel who gave his heart to God in devotion. Devotion is giving your all for something you care about. Samuel let God's love fill his life. Even when others teased him for it, Samuel stuck by his faith.

Samuel heard God's voice. At first, he didn't realize who was speaking! But he did not ignore the call. He opened his heart and God spoke. Sometimes life can be so busy, we don't even hear God. When we give up everything else to listen to God, we are blessed and good things happen. That is what devotion is all about.

David

(1 SAMUEL 16-17)

David was the youngest of his family. He grew up loving God. He also loved being a shepherd. He was always taking care of his father's flock.

A prophet named Samuel came to their town.

God told Samuel, "Go to the home of a man named Jesse. I have chosen one of his sons to be the new king of Israel."

One by one, Jesse presented his sons while David was in the field. God did not approve of any of them.

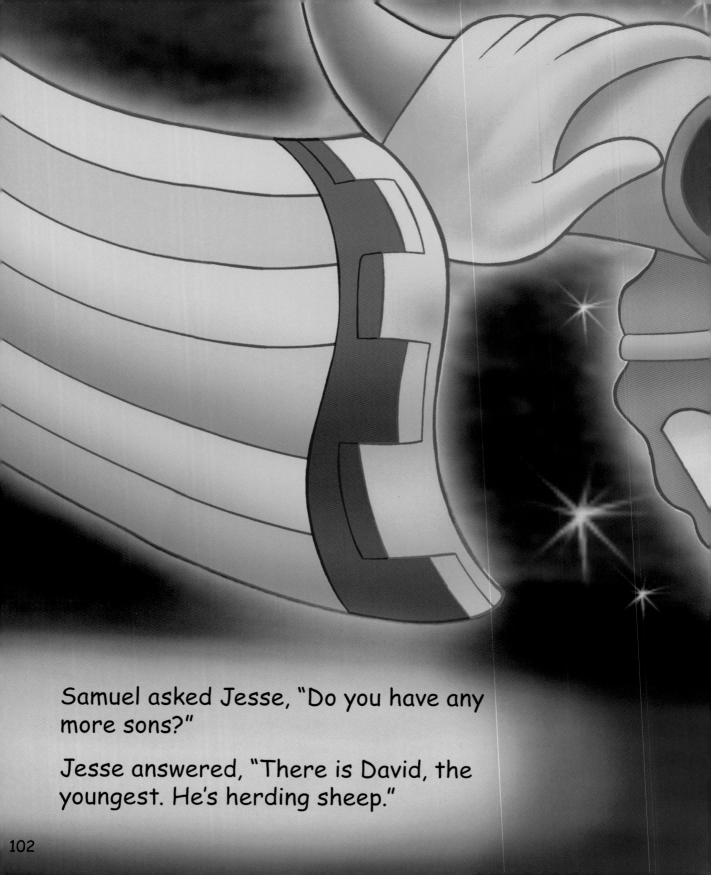

Samuel asked Jesse, "Do you have any more sons?"

Jesse answered, "There is David, the youngest. He's herding sheep."

Samuel sent for David.

As David came running up, God spoke to Samuel. He said, "Anoint him. He is the one I have chosen."

God was with David as he grew up.

One day the Philistines attacked Israel.
David's brothers left for battle. Their
father sent David to check on them.

David found his brothers in the army camp. An enemy named Goliath was teasing them from across the field. Goliath was a giant! The soldiers were afraid.

But David got angry. "He is laughing at God's own army," he said. "I'll fight him!"

David went to a nearby brook. He chose five smooth stones. He put them in his shepherd's bag. Then he ran back to Goliath.

"I'm ready to fight!" David shouted.

But Goliath just laughed. "Am I a dog? Are you going to throw stones at me?"

David answered, "You may have a sword and spear. But I come with the Lord God on my side."

David reached in his bag. He grabbed a stone and put it in his slingshot. He aimed and hit Goliath right in the forehead. Goliath fell over and hit the ground.

David was only a shepherd boy. But his love of God gave him the courage to fight. Now he had beaten Goliath, the giant. God was with him.

114

DAVID - COURAGE

David was only a boy. Yet David showed that size is not what counts. His brothers were afraid. David was afraid, too. But he had the courage to fight Goliath because he trusted in the Lord.

God honored this courage.

The Lord can do anything! David knew God takes care of those who believe. Take courage in God. You can do the impossible, too.

Josiah

(2 KINGS 22:1-20 / 23:1-4, 19-25)

Josiah was eight years old when he became king. He did not care about riches or fame. He loved God. He spent his time in God's temple. But at this time, the temple was a mess! No one seemed to care about God anymore.

So Josiah decided to clean the temple. He ordered workers to clear out the rooms. While they were working, one of the men found a scroll. It was old and dusty. Josiah realized it was God's rules. They had been lost a long time.

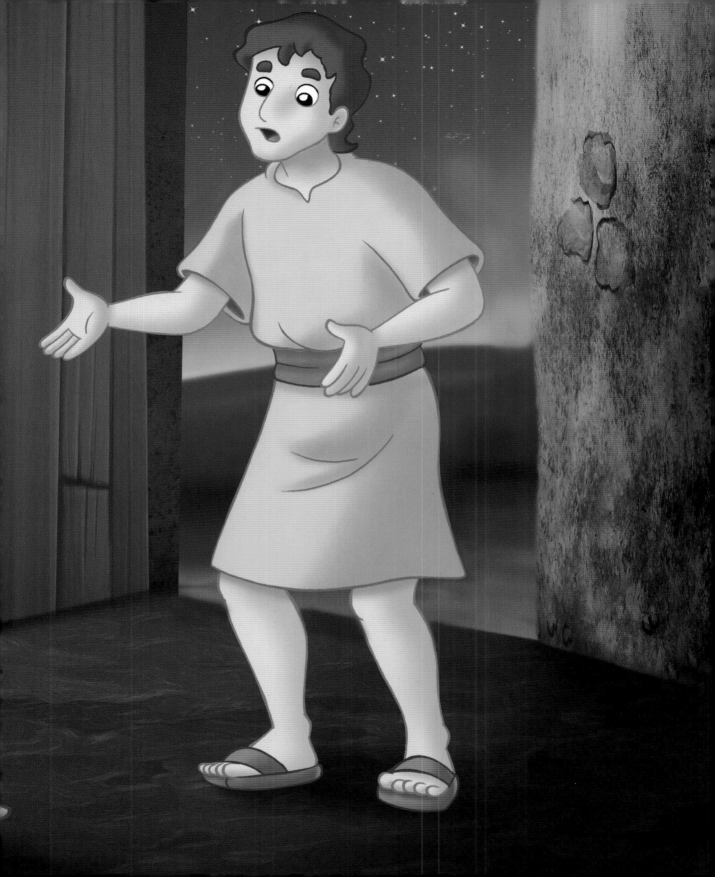

Josiah was sorry the people had forgotten
God's rules. He knew he had to do something.
So Josiah hired a group of men. "Find the best
wood and the finest stone," he said. "We're
going to repair the Lord's house!"

While the builders worked on the temple, Josiah read the scroll. Hilkiah the priest was happy. He knew they had found something very special. God's rules had been lost for a long time. But now they had been found like a precious treasure.

"These are God's laws," Josiah told Hilkiah. "We should read these to everyone! Then all the people will know how to obey the Lord."

Josiah called for a meeting. The people were curious—they poured into the temple. Then the priest took out the scroll. As he read the rules of God, the people hushed.

After the priest had finished reading, Josiah stepped forward. He began to pray, "Holy God, your people are here before you. We want to make a promise. From now on, we will follow your rules. We promise to obey you and you alone."

Josiah decided to celebrate. For the first time after many years, the people held Passover. This was a special festival in honor of God. They prayed and sang hymns. Josiah was full of joy to see the people reunite with God.

Josiah was a wonderful king. He remained loyal to the true King of kings. While others disobeyed God, Josiah kept God in his heart. He rebuilt the temple. And Josiah shared God's laws with others. He wanted everyone to know the joy of God.

JOSIAH - LOYALTY

Josiah showed loyalty to God. Loyalty is staying true, even when it's easier to turn away. Josiah didn't care about riches and fame. He wanted to be close to God. Josiah was sad to see the people stray away from God. So when Josiah found God's rules, it was a time of joy. He shared the words with everyone. Josiah showed loyalty to his people. He wanted God to look down on them with love.

Jesus
as a Boy

(LUKE 2:4-7, 40-52)

Just like you and me, Jesus was a child, too! But he was no ordinary child. There was something special about Jesus.

135

Jesus was born on a starry night in Bethlehem. He was born in a stable near the animals. His parents, Mary and Joseph, were happy to welcome him. Even the angels worshiped him. They knew that Jesus was the Son of God.

Jesus was a busy boy. He loved to help Joseph with his carpentry. He loved to help his mother, too. But most of all, Jesus loved to learn about God. He grew wiser everyday.

When Jesus was 12 years old, he went on a trip with his parents. They were going to Jerusalem for Passover. Passover was a special festival to give God thanks. Jesus could hardly wait.

When the festival was over, Mary and Joseph headed home with a crowd of people. Suddenly they looked around for Jesus. Where was he?

Not a single person they asked had seen Jesus. They ran back and forth on the road looking for him. Finally they turned back towards Jerusalem. Jesus' parents were very worried.

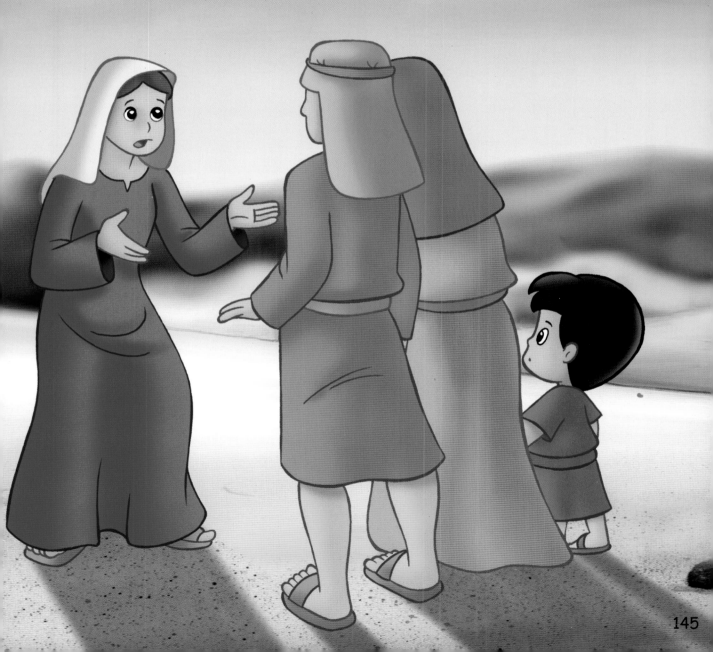

After three days, they finally found Jesus. He was in the temple learning and teaching others about God. Even the elders were asking him questions. Everyone was amazed by his wisdom.

Mary and Joseph hugged Jesus. Then Jesus asked them, "Didn't you know I would be in my Father's house?" Mary was proud of her boy. She thanked God that Jesus understood who he was.

Jesus learned more about his Father God everyday. Knowing God made him wise.

JESUS AS A BOY - WISDOM

Jesus was God's son. God's temple was Jesus' home, too. He loved to go there and learn. But Jesus did not just want to be smart. He didn't just want to know things. He wanted to know God. Jesus knew the only way to understand God was through wisdom. Wisdom is knowing things with the heart. When we read the Bible, pray, or worship in church, we will know God, too. God gives wisdom to those who seek him.

The Children and Jesus

(MARK 10:13-16; MATTHEW 19:19, 22:37-39; MATTHEW 13:1-9, 18-21; LUKE 15:3-7, JOHN 10:14-15; LUKE 6:27-28, MATTHEW 21:22, 6:9-14; MATTHEW 6:25-26; JOHN 13:34-35)

Jesus said, "Let the little children come to me and do not hinder them, for the kingdom of God belongs to such as these."

When Jesus was alive on earth, he loved to be with children! He blessed them and played with them. Jesus admired their pure hearts. His arms were always open for them.

154

Jesus taught children to love one another.
We can please him by loving our parents.
We can please him by loving our
brothers and sisters. The more we
love, the more we please God.

Jesus was a storyteller. One time he told a story about a farmer planting seeds. Some seeds fell onto rocky ground. These seeds didn't grow. Other seeds fell onto good soil. They grew big and tall. God's word is like a seed. It will grow inside a good heart.

Children are special to Jesus because they all belong to God. The Bible tells us that Jesus is our shepherd. We are his flock! If one of his little sheep is lost, Jesus will go out to find the lost one.

Praying is one of the best ways to feel close to Jesus. We can tell him anything! We can ask God to bless us. Sometimes the best prayers are when we ask God to bless others.

When we pray with an open heart, Jesus is listening. We may not see him with our eyes. We may not hear him with our ears. But we can know he is with us. Jesus lives inside our hearts.

Jesus doesn't want us to worry. "Look at the birds and butterflies," he said. "They don't worry because God takes care of them." God takes care of us, too. Share your joy with others, and you'll share the joy of Jesus.

Jesus loves us. Share his love with others. The more we love each other, the more we become like Jesus.

THE CHILDREN AND JESUS – LOVE

Jesus wants to be a part of our lives. He loves us! In his time, Jesus opened his arms to children. Today, we can still run to Jesus. We can pray. We can read the Bible. We can go to church. We can love each other. We can tell people about Jesus. Each time we do one of these things, it is like giving Jesus a hug. We can be close to him simply by loving people around us. Jesus' life is about love. Share this love with others!

The Boy with Bread and Fish

(JOHN 6:1-13)

Sometimes the simplest act of kindness can be the most important. Sometimes the smallest child can make the biggest difference. The boy with bread and fish is a good example.

One day a little boy left on a trip with his family. They were on their way to see Jesus teach. The boy grabbed some bread and fish and put it in his basket. After all, it would make a nice picnic when they got hungry.

The boy spotted Jesus on the hill. There were thousands of people sitting on the grassy hill. The boy picked out a good spot and sat down to listen. Jesus told story after story. He used stories to teach the people about right and wrong. Jesus filled the people's hearts with hope.

Sometimes people would come up to Jesus. He never turned them away. Instead, he prayed with them. He blessed the poor and the sick and the crippled. Each one of them was healed through Jesus.

The sky was beginning to darken. Jesus' disciples started to worry. "Jesus," they told him, "It is late. These people need to eat." Jesus told his disciples to feed them right away. "But we have no food!" they replied.

The boy who had been sitting quietly in the crowd stood up. He walked over to Jesus with his basket. "I have some bread and fish," he said. "It isn't much. But will it help feed the hungry people?"

Jesus looked down at the boy and
smiled. He took the boy's food and
gave thanks to God. Then he broke
the bread and fish into pieces. He
handed them to his disciples and
told them to pass the food around.

It was a miracle! Jesus kept giving out small pieces of bread and fish until everybody was fed. The people ate until their bellies were full. In fact, there were enough leftover pieces of bread and fish to fill 12 baskets! Jesus was pleased by the boy's generous gift of his small lunch.

The little boy not only helped feed thousands, he also helped Jesus teach a lesson. He showed that giving a little can go a long way. Jesus blessed his small gift and multiplied it. When we give what we have, we are part of God's miracle!

THE BOY WITH BREAD AND FISH – GENEROSITY

Generosity is giving up your own needs for the needs of others. The boy only had a few loaves of bread and some fish. He could easily have kept them for his own family. But he found joy in sharing with others. When Jesus saw his generosity, he used the boy's lunch to do a miracle! Jesus made sure the boy's small offering would grow. Thousands of people were fed. Just think what can happen when we share with others! Our acts of giving will grow and grow. One kind gift can inspire even more kind gifts. And you can be sure Jesus will bless each one.

BIBLE REFERENCE

ISAAC - TRUST

GENESIS 21:1-4

The LORD was good to Sarah and kept his promise. Although Abraham was very old, Sarah had a son exactly at the time God had said. Abraham named his son Isaac, and when the boy was eight days old, Abraham circumcised him, just as the LORD had commanded.

GENESIS 22:1-19

Some years later God decided to test Abraham, so he spoke to him.

Abraham answered, "Here I am, LORD."

The LORD said, "Go get Isaac, your only son, the one you dearly love! Take him to the land of Moriah, and I will show you a mountain where you must sacrifice him to me on the fires of an altar." So Abraham got up early the next morning and chopped wood for the fire. He put a saddle on his donkey and left with Isaac and two servants for the place where God had told him to go.

Three days later Abraham looked off in the distance and saw the place.

He told his servants, "Stay here with the donkey, while my son and I go over there to worship. We will come back."

Abraham put the wood on Isaac's shoulder, but he carried the hot coals and the knife. As the two of them walked along, Isaac said, "Father, we have the coals and the wood, but where is the lamb for the sacrifice?"

"My son," Abraham answered, "God will provide the lamb."

The two of them walked on, and when they reached the place that God had told him about, Abraham built an altar and placed the wood on it. Next, he tied up his son and put him on the wood. He then took the knife and got ready to kill his son. But the LORD's angel shouted from heaven, "Abraham! Abraham!"

"Here I am!" he answered.

"Don't hurt the boy or harm him in any way!" the angel said. "Now I know that you truly obey God, because you were willing to offer him your only son."

Abraham looked up and saw a ram caught by its horns in the bushes. So he took the ram and sacrificed it in place of his son.

Abraham named that place "The LORD Will Provide." And even now people say, "On the mountain of the LORD it will be provided." The LORD's angel called out from heaven a second time: You were willing to offer the LORD your only son, and so he makes you this solemn promise, "I will bless you and give you such a large family, that someday your descendants will be more numerous than the stars in the sky or the grains of sand along the beach. They will defeat their enemies and take over the cities where their enemies live. You have obeyed me, and so you and your descendants will be a blessing to all nations on earth."

Abraham and Isaac

went back to the servants who had come with him, and they returned to Abraham's home in Beersheba.

MIRIAM - INTELLIGENCE

EXODUS 2:1-9

A man from the Levi tribe married a woman from the same tribe, and she later had a baby boy. He was a beautiful child, and she kept him inside for three months. But when she could no longer keep him hidden, she made a basket out of reeds and covered it with tar. She put him in the basket and placed it in the tall grass along the edge of the Nile River. The baby's older sister stood off at a distance to see what would happen to him. About that time one of the king's daughters came down to take a bath in the river, while her servant women walked along the river bank. She saw the basket in the tall grass and sent one of the young women to pull it out of the water. When the king's daughter opened the basket, she saw the baby and felt sorry for him because he was crying. She said, " This must be one of the Hebrew babies." At once the baby's older sister came up and asked, " Do you want me to get a Hebrew woman to take care of the baby for you?"

" Yes," the king's daughter answered.

So the girl brought the baby's mother, and the king's daughter told her, " Take care of this child, and I will pay you."

The baby's mother carried him home and took care of him.

MOSES - DETERMINATION

EXODUS 2:1-10

A man from the Levi tribe married a woman from the same tribe, and she later had a baby boy. He was a beautiful child, and she kept him inside for three months. But when she could no longer keep him hidden, she made a basket out of reeds and covered it with tar. She put him in the basket and placed it in the tall grass along the edge of the Nile River. The baby's older sister stood off at a distance to see what would happen to him. About that time one of the king's daughters came down to take a bath in the river, while her servant women walked along the river bank. She saw the basket in the tall grass and sent one of the young women to pull it out of the water. When the king's daughter opened the basket, she saw the baby and felt sorry for him because he was crying. She said, " This must be one of the Hebrew babies." At once the baby's older sister came up and asked, " Do you want me to get a Hebrew woman to take care of the baby for you?"

" Yes," the king's daughter answered.

So the girl brought the baby's mother, and the king's daughter told her, " Take care of this child, and I will pay you."

The baby's mother carried him home and took care of him. And when he was old enough, she took him to the king's daughter, who adopted him. She named him Moses because she said, " I pulled him out of the water."

NAAMAN'S SERVANT GIRL - COMPASSION

2 KINGS 5:1-14

Naaman was the commander of the Syrian army. The LORD had helped him and his troops defeat their enemies, so the king of Syria respected Naaman very much. Naaman was a brave soldier, but he had leprosy. One day while the Syrian troops were raiding Israel, they captured a girl, and she became a servant of Naaman's wife. Some time later the girl said, "If your husband Naaman would go to the prophet in Samaria, he would be cured of his leprosy."

When Naaman told the king what the girl had said, the king replied, "Go ahead! I will give you a letter to take to the king of Israel."

Naaman left and took along seven hundred fifty pounds of silver, one hundred fifty pounds of gold, and ten new outfits. He also carried the letter to the king of Israel. It said, "I am sending my servant Naaman to you. Would you cure him of his leprosy?"

When the king of Israel read the letter, he tore his clothes in fear and shouted, "That Syrian king believes I can cure this man of leprosy! Does he think I'm God with power over life and death? He must be trying to pick a fight with me."

As soon as Elisha the prophet heard what had happened, he sent the Israelite king this message: "Why are you so afraid? Send the man to me, so that he will know there is a prophet in Israel." Naaman left with his horses and chariots and stopped at the door of Elisha's house. Elisha sent someone outside to say to him, "Go wash seven times in the Jordan River. Then you'll be completely cured."

But Naaman stormed off, grumbling, "Why couldn't he come out and talk to me? I thought for sure he would stand in front of me and pray to the LORD his God, then wave his hand over my skin and cure me. What about the Abana River or the Pharpar River? Those rivers in Damascus are just as good as any river in Israel. I could have washed in them and been cured." His servants went over to him and said, "Sir, if the prophet had told you to do something difficult, you would have done it. So why don't you do what he said? Go wash and be cured."

Naaman walked down to the Jordan; he waded out into the water and stooped down in it seven times, just as Elisha had told him. Right away, he was cured, and his skin became as smooth as a child's.

SAMUEL - DEVOTION

1 SAMUEL 1:9-28

When the sacrifice had been offered, and they had eaten the meal, Hannah got up and went to pray. Eli was sitting in his chair near the door to the place of worship. Hannah was brokenhearted and was crying as she prayed, "LORD All-Powerful, I am your servant, but I am so miserable! Please let me have a son. I will give him to you for as long as he lives, and his hair will never be cut." Hannah prayed silently to the LORD for a long time. But her lips were moving, and Eli thought she was drunk. "How long are you going to stay drunk?" he asked. "Sober up!"

"Sir, please don't think I'm no good!" Hannah answered. "I'm not drunk, and I haven't been drinking. But I do feel miserable and terribly upset. I've been praying all this time, telling the LORD about my problems."

Eli replied, "You may go home now and stop worrying. I'm sure the God of Israel will answer your prayer."

"Sir, thank you for being so kind to me," Hannah said. Then she left, and after eating something, she felt much better.

Elkanah and his family got up early the next morning and worshiped the LORD. Then they went back home to Ramah. Later the LORD blessed Elkanah and Hannah with a son. She named him Samuel because she had asked the LORD for him.

Hannah Gives Samuel to the LORD

The next time Elkanah and his family went to offer their yearly sacrifice, he took along a gift that he had promised to give to the LORD. But Hannah stayed home, because she had told Elkanah, "Samuel and I won't go until he's old enough for me to stop nursing him. Then I'll give him to the LORD, and he can stay there at Shiloh for the rest of his life."

"You know what's best," Elkanah said. "Stay here until it's time to stop nursing him. I'm sure the LORD will help you do what you have promised." Hannah did not go to Shiloh until she stopped nursing Samuel. When it was the time of year to go to Shiloh again, Hannah and Elkanah took Samuel to the LORD's house. They brought along a three-year-old bull, a twenty-pound sack of flour, and a clay jar full of wine. Hannah and Elkanah offered the bull as a sacrifice, then brought the little boy to Eli. "Sir," Hannah said, "a few years ago I stood here beside you and asked the LORD to give me a child. Here he is! The LORD gave me just what I asked for. Now I am giving him to the LORD, and he will be the LORD's servant for as long as he lives."

1 SAMUEL 3:1-19

Samuel served the LORD by helping Eli the priest, who was by that time almost blind. In those days, the LORD hardly ever spoke directly to people, and he did not appear to them in dreams very often. But one night, Eli was asleep in his room, and Samuel was sleeping on a mat near the sacred chest in the LORD's house. They had not been asleep very long when the LORD called out Samuel's name. "Here I am!" Samuel answered. Then he ran to Eli and said, "Here I am. What do you want?"

"I didn't call you," Eli answered. "Go back to bed."
Samuel went back.

Again the LORD called out Samuel's name. Samuel got up and went to Eli. "Here I am," he said. "What do you want?"

Eli told him, "Son, I didn't call you. Go back to sleep."

The LORD had not spoken to Samuel before, and Samuel did not recognize the voice. When the LORD called out his name for the third time, Samuel went to Eli again and said, "Here I am. What do you want?"

Eli finally realized that it was the LORD who was speaking to Samuel. So he said, "Go back and lie down! If someone speaks to you again, answer, `I'm listening, LORD. What do you want me to do?'

Once again Samuel went back and lay down.

The LORD then stood beside Samuel and called out as he had done before, "Samuel! Samuel!"

"I'm listening," Samuel answered. "What do you want me to do?"

The LORD said:

Samuel, I am going to do something in Israel that will shock everyone who hears about it! I will punish Eli and his family, just as I promised. He knew that his sons refused to respect me, and he let them get away with it, even though I said I would punish his family forever. I warned Eli that sacrifices or offerings could never make things right! His family has done too many disgusting things. The next morning, Samuel got up and opened the doors to the LORD's house. He was afraid to tell Eli what the LORD had said. But Eli told him, "Samuel, my boy, come here!"

"Here I am," Samuel answered.

Eli said, "What did God say to you? Tell me everything. I pray that God will punish you terribly if you don't tell me every word he said!"

Samuel told Eli everything. Then Eli said, "He is the LORD, and he will do what's right."

The LORD Helps Samuel

As Samuel grew up, the LORD helped him and made everything Samuel said come true.

DAVID - COURAGE

1 SAMUEL 16:14-23

The Spirit of the LORD had left King Saul, and he was sad. Saul said, "Find me someone who is good at playing the harp and bring him here."

"A man named Jesse who lives in Bethlehem has a son who can play the harp," one official said, "and the LORD is with him."

Saul sent a message to Jesse, saying, "Tell your son David to leave your sheep and come here to me." David went to Saul and started working for him. Saul liked him. David would play his harp. Saul would relax and feel better.

1 SAMUEL 17:1-26, 32-50

The Philistines got ready for war and brought their troops together to attack. The Philistine army had a hero named Goliath who was over nine feet tall. Goliath went out and shouted to the army of Israel, "Why are you lining up for battle? I'm the best soldier in our army. Choose your best soldier to come out and fight me!"

One day, Jesse told David, "Hurry and take this sack of roasted grain and these ten loaves of bread to your brothers at the army camp and find out how they are doing."

David obeyed his father. He got up early the next morning and loaded the supplies and started off. He reached the army camp just as the soldiers were taking their places and shouting the battle cry. The army of Israel and the Philistine army stood there facing each other.

David left his things and ran up to the battle line to ask his brothers if they were well. While David was talking with them, Goliath came out from the line of Philistines and started boasting as usual. David heard him. When the Israelite soldiers saw Goliath, they were scared and ran off.

David asked some soldiers standing nearby, "Who does that worthless Philistine think he is? He's making fun of the army of the living God!"

Some soldiers overheard David talking, so they told Saul what David had said. Saul sent for David, and David came. "Your Majesty," he said, "this Philistine shouldn't turn us into cowards. I'll go out and fight him myself!"

Saul had his own military clothes and armor put on David, and he gave David a bronze helmet to wear. David strapped on a sword and tried to walk around, but he was not used to wearing those things.

"I can't move with all this stuff on," David said. "I'm just not used to it."

David took off the armor and picked up his shepherd's stick. He went out to a stream and picked up five smooth rocks and put them in his leather bag. Then with his sling in his hand, he went straight toward Goliath.

When Goliath saw that David was just a healthy, good-looking boy, he made fun of him. "Do you think I'm a dog?" Goliath asked. "Is that why you've come after me with a stick?"

David answered, "You've come out to fight me with a sword and a spear and a dagger. But I've come out to fight you in the name of the LORD All-Powerful. He is the God of Israel's army."

David ran toward him. He put a rock in his sling and swung the sling around by its straps. When he let go of one strap, the rock flew out and hit Goliath, and he fell facedown on the ground. David defeated Goliath with a sling and a rock.

JOSIAH - LOYALTY

2 KINGS 22:1-20

Josiah was eight years old when he became king of Judah, and he ruled thirty-one years from Jerusalem. His mother Jedidah was the daughter of Adaiah from Bozkath. Josiah always obeyed the LORD, just as his ancestor David had done.

After Josiah had been king for eighteen years, he told Shaphan, one of his highest officials: Go to the LORD's temple and ask Hilkiah the high priest to collect from the guards all the money that the people have donated. Have Hilkiah give it to the men supervising the repairs to the temple. They can use some of the money to pay the workers, and with the rest of it they can buy wood and stone for the repair work. They are honest, so we won't ask them to keep track of the money.

While Shaphan was at the temple, Hilkiah handed him a book and said, "Look what I found here in the temple--The Book of God's Law."

Shaphan read it, then went back to Josiah and reported, "Your officials collected the money in the temple and gave it to the men supervising the repairs. But there's something else, Your Majesty. The priest Hilkiah gave me this book." Then Shaphan read it out loud.

When Josiah heard what was in The Book of God's Law, he tore his clothes in sorrow. At once he called together Hilkiah, Shaphan, Ahikam son of Shaphan, Achbor son of Micaiah, and his own servant Asaiah. He said, "The LORD must be furious with me and everyone else in Judah, because our ancestors did not obey the laws written in this book. Go find out what the LORD wants us to do."

The five men left right away and went to talk with Huldah the prophet. Her husband was Shallum, who was in charge of the king's clothes. Huldah lived in the northern part of Jerusalem, and when they met in her home, she said: You were sent here by King Josiah, and this is what the LORD God of Israel says to him: "Josiah, I am the LORD! And I will see to it that this country and everyone living in it will be destroyed. It will happen just as this book says. The people of Judah have rejected me. They have offered sacrifices to foreign gods and have worshiped their own idols. I cannot stand it any longer. I am furious.

"Josiah, listen to what I am going to do. I noticed how sad you were when you read that this country and its people would be completely wiped out. You even tore your clothes in sorrow, and I heard you cry. So I will let you die in peace, before I destroy this place."

The men left and took Huldah's answer back to Josiah.

2 KINGS 23:1-4, 19-25

King Josiah called together the older leaders of Judah and Jerusalem. Then he went to the LORD's temple, together with the people of Judah and Jerusalem, the priests, and the prophets. Finally, when everybody was there, he read aloud The Book of God's Law [a] that had been found in the temple. After Josiah had finished reading, he stood by one of the columns. He asked the people to promise in the LORD's name to faithfully obey the LORD and to follow his commands. The people agreed to do everything written in the book.

Josiah told Hilkiah the priest, the assistant priests, and the guards at the temple door to go into the temple and bring out the things used to worship Baal, Asherah, and the stars. Josiah had these things burned in Kidron Valley just outside Jerusalem, and he had the ashes carried away to the town of Bethel.

Some of the Israelite kings had made the LORD angry by building pagan shrines all over Israel. So Josiah sent troops to destroy these shrines just as he had done to the one in Bethel. He killed the priests who served at them and burned their bones on the altars.

After all that, Josiah went back to Jerusalem.

Josiah and the People of Judah Celebrate Passover

Josiah told the people of Judah, "Celebrate Passover in honor of the LORD your God, just as it says in The Book of God's Law." This festival had not been celebrated in this way since kings ruled Israel and Judah. But in Josiah's eighteenth year as king of Judah, everyone came to Jerusalem to celebrate Passover.

Josiah got rid of every disgusting person and thing in Judah and Jerusalem--including magicians, fortunetellers, and idols. He did his best to obey every law written in the book that the priest Hilkiah found in the LORD's temple. No other king before or after Josiah tried as hard as he did to obey the Law of Moses.

JESUS AS A BOY

LUKE 2:4-7, 40-52

Joseph went up from the town of Nazareth in Galilee to Judea, to Bethlehem the town of David, because he belonged to the house and line of David. He went there to register with Mary, who was pledged to be married to him and was expecting a child. While they were there, the time came for the baby to be born, and she gave birth to her firstborn, a son. She wrapped him in cloths and placed him in a manger, because there was no room for them in the inn. And the child grew and became strong; he was filled with wisdom, and the grace of God was upon him.

Every year his parents went to Jerusalem for the Feast of the Passover. When he was twelve years old, they went up to the Feast, according to the custom. After the Feast was over, while his parents were returning home, the boy Jesus stayed behind in Jerusalem, but they were unaware of it. Thinking he was in their company, they traveled on for a day. Then they began looking for him among their relatives and friends.

When they did not find him, they went back to Jerusalem to look for him. After three days they found him in the temple courts, sitting among the teachers, listening to them and asking them questions. Everyone who heard him was amazed at his understanding and his answers. When his parents saw him, they were astonished. His mother said to him, "Son, why have you treated us like this? Your father and I have been anxiously searching for you."

"Why were you searching for me?" he asked. "Didn't you know I had to be in my Father's house?" But they did not understand what he was saying to them.

Then he went down to Nazareth with them and was obedient to them. But his mother treasured all these things in her heart. And Jesus grew in wisdom and stature, and in favor with God and men.

THE CHILDREN AND JESUS – LOVE

MARK 10:13-16

People were bringing little children to Jesus for him to place his hands on them, but the disciples rebuked them. When Jesus saw this, he was indignant. He said to them, "Let the little children come to me, and do not hinder them, for the kingdom of God belongs to such as these. Truly I tell you, anyone who will not receive the kingdom of God like a little child will never enter it." And he took the children in his arms, placed his hands on them and blessed them.

MATTHEW 19:19, 22:37-39

Jesus replied, "Love your neighbor as yourself."

Jesus answered, "Love the Lord your God with all your heart, soul, and mind. This is the first and most important commandment. The second most important commandment is like this one. And it is, 'Love others as much as you love yourself.'"

MATTHEW 13:1-9, 18-21

Jesus taught them many things by using stories. He said: A farmer went out to scatter seed in a field. While the farmer was scattering the seed, some of it fell along the road and was eaten by birds. Other seeds fell on thin, rocky ground and quickly started growing because the soil wasn't very deep. But when the sun came up, the plants were scorched and dried up, because they did not have enough roots. Some other seeds fell where thorn bushes grew up and choked the plants. But a few seeds did fall on good ground where the plants produced a hundred or sixty or thirty times as much as was scattered.

Now listen to the meaning of the story about the farmer:

The seeds that fell along the road are the people who hear the message about the kingdom, but don't understand it. Then the evil one comes and snatches the message from their hearts. The seeds that fell on rocky ground are the people who gladly hear the message and accept it right away. But they don't have deep roots, and they don't last very long. As soon as life gets hard or the message gets them in trouble, they give up.

The seeds that fell among the thorn bushes are also people who hear the message. But they start worrying about the needs of this life and are fooled by the desire to get rich. So the message gets choked out, and they never produce anything. The seeds that fell on good ground are the people who hear and understand the message. They produce as much as a hundred or sixty or thirty times what was planted.

LUKE 15:3-7, JOHN 10:14-15

Then Jesus told them this story:

If any of you has a hundred sheep, and one of them gets lost, what will you do? Won't you leave the ninety-nine in the field and go look for the lost sheep until you find it? And when you find it, you will be so glad that you will put it on your shoulder and carry it home. Then you will call in your friends and neighbors and say, "Let's celebrate! I've found my lost sheep."

Jesus said, "In the same way there is more happiness in heaven because of one sinner who turns to God than over ninety-nine good people who don't need to."

I am the good shepherd. I know my sheep, and they know me. Just as the Father knows me, I know the Father, and I give up my life for my sheep.

LUKE 6:27-28, MATTHEW 21:22, 6:9-14

Love your enemies, and be good to everyone who hates you. Ask God to bless anyone who curses you, and pray for everyone who is cruel to you.

If you have faith when you pray, you will be given whatever you ask for.

You should pray like this: Our Father in heaven, help us to honor your name. Come and set up your kingdom, so that everyone on earth will obey you, as you are obeyed in heaven. Give us our food for today. Forgive us for doing wrong, as we forgive others. Keep us from being tempted and protect us from evil. If you forgive others for the wrongs they do to you, your Father in heaven will forgive you. But if you don't forgive others, your Father will not forgive your sins.

MATTHEW 6:25-26

I tell you not to worry about your life. Don't worry about having something to eat, drink, or wear. Isn't life more than food or clothing? Look at the birds in the sky! They don't plant or harvest. They don't even store grain in barns. Yet your Father in heaven takes care of them. Aren't you worth more than birds?

JOHN 13:34-35

Jesus said, "A new command I give you: Love one another. As I have loved you, so you must love one another. By this everyone will know that you are my disciples, if you love one another."

THE BOY WITH BREAD AND FISH
JOHN 6:1-13

Jesus crossed to the far shore of the Sea of Galilee (that is, the Sea of Tiberias), and a great crowd of people followed him because they saw the miraculous signs he had performed on the sick. Then Jesus went up on a mountainside and sat down with his disciples. The Jewish Passover Feast was near.

When Jesus looked up and saw a great crowd coming toward him, he said to Philip, "Where shall we buy bread for these people to eat?" He asked this only to test him, for he already had in mind what he was going to do.

Philip answered him, "Eight months' wages would not buy enough bread for each one to have a bite!"

Another of his disciples, Andrew, Simon Peter's brother, spoke up, "Here is a boy with five small barley loaves and two small fish, but how far will they go among so many?"

Jesus said, "Have the people sit down. "There was plenty of grass in that place, and the men sat down, about five thousand of them. Jesus then took the loaves, gave thanks, and distributed to those who were seated as much as they wanted. He did the same with the fish.

When they had all had enough to eat, he said to his disciples, "Gather the pieces that are left over. Let nothing be wasted." So they gathered them and filled twelve baskets with the pieces of the five barley loaves left over by those who had eaten.

After the people saw the miraculous sign that Jesus did, they began to say, "Surely this is the Prophet who is to come into the world."Jesus, knowing that they intended to come and make him king by force, withdrew again to a mountain by himself.